The
Take-Charge Teacher

5 Steps to Create Effective Classroom Routines Your Students Will Actually Do

BY KATRINA AYRES

Previously published in eBook format as

CLASSROOM MANAGEMENT STRATEGIES THAT WORK:
STRATEGY 1- CLASSROOM ROUTINES

MOLDENHAUER

Books and eBooks by Katrina Ayres

All The Ways I Screwed Up My First Year of Teaching
And How You Can Avoid Doing It, Too, 2012

Classroom Management Strategies That Work:
Strategy 1 - Classroom Routines, 2014

The Classroom Teacher's Coloring Book, 2015

The Affirmations and Encouragement Coloring Book
For Grown-Ups, 2015

5-Minute Classroom Management Hints:
37 Proven Ways to Manage Your Classroom and Keep Your Sanity, 2016

The Take-Charge Teacher:
5 Steps to Create Effective Classroom Routines Your Students Will Actually Do

Previously published in eBook format as *Classroom Management Strategies That Work:*
Strategy 1 - Classroom Routines

Copyright © 2016 Katrina Ayres

ISBN: 1533600325
ISBN-13: 978-1533600325

Author photo by Kate Singh, aevuminages.com

Illustrations by Andreea Mironiuc, andreeamironiuc.com

CONTENTS

Is This Book For Me?

This book is for you if you are a K-12 classroom teacher or are preparing to become one, and you want a positive, well-run, organized classroom. This book is for you if you care deeply about your students and want to provide them with the best possible education instead of just getting by with the bare minimum. This book is for you if you do not want to be one of the thousands of teachers who struggle every day with your students and end up quitting or losing your job before you even finish paying off your school loans.

This book is for you if you are willing to invest the time and effort to proactively prevent problems in your classroom instead of waiting for something to go wrong and then reacting; if you want to take the time to develop a plan that will really work instead of guessing, hoping, and praying everything will turn out okay. This book will not be a good match for you if you just want to roll along spontaneously and handle things as they come up.

In this book we are going to get specific. We are going to go deep. We are going to think things through and make plans. We are going to write things down and be prepared. This is an interactive book. This means in order to get the results you want from this book, you will need to *interact* with it. If you don't want to do any of the activities, please don't buy this book.

So let's see if this really is the right book for you, right now. Are you willing to jump right in to the first activity? If so, turn the page!

Activity #1 ✍

Estimated Time = 1 minute

Materials

- Pencil or Pen
- Paper

Please write down five things that worry you about student behavior in your classroom (or your future classroom, if you're just starting out.) I know you may also be worried about other things, such as your curriculum, Common Core, or parent communication. These are important, too. However, the topic of this interactive guide is classroom management, so I'd like you to focus only on student behavior.

What five things have you seen in classrooms you hope to never see in yours? Please do not just do this in your head—actually write it down. (If you don't have paper, you may want to create an electronic note, or text or email the list to yourself. But put it into words!)

What Was On Your List?

Each week, I send out a classroom management hint called the Monday Morning Sanity Boost. I recently asked my readers to send me their top questions about classroom management. Here is what they asked:

- How can I rein in excessive talking and general constant chatter? Students who can't help but blurt out whatever is on their mind? Keep kids quiet while walking in line?
- There's no respect! What can I do?
- The students destroy books and furniture. How can I stop them?
- What about all the homework excuses?
- How can I deal with inappropriate use of electronics?
- How can I get the students' attention? How can I get back the attention of the class when I have "lost" them?
- How can I deal with students whose cognitive or emotional ability is not anywhere near their actual age? 16 year-olds with the emotional maturity level of a 4 year-old? Students who are two years behind?
- How can I work with individual students and still give the rest of the group the attention they need?
- What about if I don't have administrative support?
- How can I reward good behavior?
- What is the best way to communicate with parents about their child's behavior?
- How can I stop repeating directions and asking kids to do things multiple times?

- What about attention-getting behavior (class clown) and other disruptive behavior from just a few students? The willfully disrespectful student who looks around the room for your reaction and the reaction of other students?
- What if students refuse to participate? How can I deal with students who pack up before class is over?
- How do you create community in your classroom? What if I don't have my own classroom?

How did these concerns match up with your list from Activity #1? My guess is you are concerned about many of the same things as my readers. When students seem to have a complete disregard for the rules, unruly behavior can make it difficult to get anything done in class, no matter how engaging the curriculum.

The stress level of teachers is through the roof. We want to do our jobs, and we know how important education is, yet many times we feel trapped and ill-equipped. New teachers are sent out into the most difficult situations, confident that their college programs have prepared them, only to find out they have not. Is it any wonder that half of all new teachers quit or are fired within their first five years?

The saddest part (to me) is the effect on our students, particularly those most at risk of failure. When there is little or no learning going on in a classroom, the effects are felt long after the school year is over. Some students never recover the academic ground they lost during that year, adding to the risk they will drop out or be excluded from school. In addition, students can develop negative habits and behaviors that make it difficult to succeed in life—habits which can be almost impossible to break after years of reinforcement and repetition.

Good teaching begins with effective classroom management, and effective classroom management begins with powerful routines. A *routine* is a systematic way your students are expected to do common activities in your class. Effective classroom routines, correctly taught to your students, can truly transform your classroom. You will be able to maintain your personal power, save hours of wasted time, and truly enjoy teaching. Let's take a few examples from the questions above.

- **How to prevent chatter and blurting out?** Proactively teach your students the "chatter level" you expect during different types of activities. (See page 34 for a list of different "chatter levels.") Will teaching about chatter make all students instantly comply with your wishes? Of course not. But it will eliminate inappropriate chatter that happens because the students are used to chattering all the time at home, and don't know anything different. It will reduce the number of students who talk and shout out to find out where the limits are. It will also give you a way to talk to the students about chatter BEFORE it becomes a problem, instead of blaming and punishing them afterward.

- **Lack of respect**—Get very clear about what you really mean when you say "respect." Today's students come from a variety of cultures and home situations. Their idea of "respect" may be totally different than yours. (More about that in Step 2.)

- **Vandalism and abuse of materials**—Do the students know how to properly care for the materials? Or are we going to leave it to chance?

- **Homework excuses**—Have you taught them how to do homework, even when there is no support at home? This can be a very illuminating class discussion, as you can well imagine.

- **Inappropriate use of electronics**—Teach a routine for the appropriate use of electronics.

- **Getting the students' attention**—Teach a routine for what to do when I ring the chimes, clap my hands, move to the "teaching position" at the front of the room, and so on.

You get the idea. And while classroom routines will not solve every classroom management issue, they are a great place to start. If you are new to teaching, the most important thing to focus on in your first year is how to systematically teach routines to your students. If you already struggle with student behavior issues, routines are usually the best way to quickly regain control.

Telling Versus Teaching

I hear and I forget. I see and I remember. I do and I understand. -
Confucius

Many teachers think they have taught classroom routines to their students, when in fact they have not. They have *told* or *explained* about classroom routines, which is not the same thing at all. As teachers, we know we can't just talk about our academic subject and expect the students to instantly understand it. Yet when it comes to behavior, many of us make the classic blunder of *telling* instead of *teaching*.

Telling and teaching are not the same. A classroom routine has only been taught when every student has demonstrated they can do it. In Step 5 I will show you the correct way to teach classroom routines to your students and ensure they actually understand them.

How to Use This Book

Would you like a book that lists a fail-safe solution for each of the classroom management questions or worries you have?

So would I.

Unfortunately, that book doesn't exist. I certainly don't have all the answers, and there is no "expert" who does. Each student is different, each teacher is different, and each situation is different. A solution that works really well for me might be a disaster in your classroom, and your favorite classroom management strategy might not be effective at all with my students. Not only that, but a technique that works well in my fourth period class may not be effective at all with my eighth period class, and the strategies that worked for me last year might not work this year.

Although you can borrow ideas from other teachers, in the end you will need to create your own routines. That is what this book is all about. In this book, I will teach you a five-step process you can use over and over to create specific solutions to specific problems you are dealing with in your classroom. I discovered this process in my own classroom 17 years ago, and it's been working for me ever since.

Each chapter explains one of the five steps of the process, gives two examples of how to do the step, and ends with an activity. I have estimated the time each activity will take, and the entire process (all five steps) can be done in approximately one hour if you just skip straight to the activities and do them. (I don't recommend you do this, of course, but I know you are busy. If you have to skip something, skip the explanations, not the activities. Remember, this is *an interactive book*!) Templates and examples are available right after each activity, as well.

Throughout the book I will follow two teachers, Brian and Karen, as they work their way through the process. I deliberately chose newer teachers for these examples because I wish I had known about this process when I first started out in the classroom. It is my hope and dream this book will find its way into the hands of new teachers and save them from making all the embarrassing and painful mistakes I made when I first started out. (If you are interested in my mistakes, you can read all about it in my first book, *All The Ways I Screwed Up My First Year of Teaching, And How You Can Avoid Doing It, Too*, available on Amazon.)

And now let's meet our two example teachers, Brian and Karen.

Brian

Brian is a second-year teacher in the small town where he grew up. He teaches third grade and has 26 students. Or he did, until one of the high-profile parents insisted the principal transfer her daughter into the other third grade early in the school year. In a town where everyone knows everyone else, this was a big embarrassment. He feels like everyone in town is watching him under a microscope.

Brian chose to teach at the elementary level because he enjoys silliness and fun. He loves to draw funny cartoons, sing goofy songs, and teach his students using stories and educational games. Some students have interpreted his creativity and sense of fun to mean they can do whatever they want. A couple of bullies have emerged who steal from other students and refuse to share classroom materials. Unfortunately, this behavior is now common in his class.

When Brian tries to reason with his students and encourage them to treat each other with respect, they ignore him and continue doing whatever they want. The noise level is always high, which is distressing to his autistic student who often put his hands over his ears, rocks, and cries. Few students turn in any work. When they do, it is low quality. Brian dreads the standardized test coming soon because he knows his students won't be prepared. He doesn't want to turn into a skill-and-drill teacher and give up his creativity, but he sees no alternative. Teaching is no longer fun, and he has started reading job listings on LinkedIn.

Karen

Karen recently graduated from college and earned her teaching credential for high school math. Before that she was a full-time mother. She's been through the school system with her own children and believes she knows what it takes to be a good teacher. Since her graduation she has been doing everything she can to prepare herself for success in her first job. She visits Pinterest boards for classroom setup and lesson plan ideas. She attends conferences when she can and asks for pointers from teachers she respects.

Since Karen didn't get a full-time job right away, she started substitute teaching. Subbing has been an eye-opener for her. The students are not as orderly and respectful as when she did her internship. She remembers a few of her own children's teachers who struggled to maintain control of their classrooms, and as she subs she sees the same thing.

A little nagging doubt starts to form inside of her. What if she's like those out-of-control teachers? What if she fails? For the first time, Karen is not as worried about getting a job as she is about the job itself.

Brian and Karen have both started to suspect there may be a little more to teaching than giving out information. They are beginning to see what happens when classroom routines are not explicitly and systematically taught to students. Brian is desperate to make changes in his classroom, and Karen wants to make sure she is well-prepared. Both of them need to learn how to teach classroom routines.

I invite you to join with Brian and Karen as they create their first classroom routines using the five-step process. But before we dig in, let's take a look at a quick overview.

Overview

The five steps to create a classroom routine are: pick your routine, envision perfection, troubleshooting, lesson planning, and teaching the routine. Let's go over each one briefly to get an idea of where this process is taking us.

Step 1—Pick Your Routine—While this may seem obvious, it's important to choose a high-leverage routine to work on. As I mentioned earlier, it will take about an hour to do the activities in this book, and you want that time to be wisely invested. There is no sense creating an elaborate routine for something your students rarely do, or for an activity that isn't likely to cause problems in your class.

Step 2—Envision Perfection—Before you can effectively teach a routine to your students, you need to know what you want them to do. If you do not give enough thought to this step you will end up with a vague routine. Vague routines lead to students pushing the limits, which can lead to anger and frustration on the part of the teacher. In this step, I will give you exercises you can use to help you be very specific with your students about what you want.

Step 3—Troubleshooting—If you take the time to figure out what could go wrong with your routine and what you will do about it, you will be better prepared with proactive solutions and appropriate consequences. This step is key to being perceived as fair by your students, which will go a long way toward getting them to go along with what you are asking them to do.

Step 4—Lesson Planning—This is where you will plan how to teach your routine, including what you will say to your students and how they will practice it. Also included in this step is an explanation of how to teach a routine to your students in the middle of the year.

Step 5—Teaching the Routine—In this step you will roll out your routine with your class. I will show you how and when to teach your routine, how often to review, and more.

Once you create a few routines using this process you will have a workable plan for how to start the school year and/or how to regain control of your class if it has gotten out of hand. I look forward to hearing about your success and possibly even seeing your routine (if you are willing to share it.) You can email me at PositiveTeachingStrategies@gmail.com.

And now let's get started!

Step 1
Pick Your Routine

It's important to systematically choose which routines to teach because it's impossible to create and explicitly teach a routine for every action your students will take. I suggest you create classroom routines for two types of events—*transitions* and *classroom activities.*

A *transition* occurs whenever your students move from one activity or place to another. Each transition offers an opportunity for your students to waste time or get out of control. For example, a simple activity such as passing out papers can be an opportunity for students to get up and walk around, talk about last weekend, dig in their desks, peek at their phones, and so on. If this happens, you will need to spend valuable instructional time regaining their attention, which may result in you sounding negative.

As you can see, this simple activity could damage you relationship with your students, waste time, and lead to even more disruptive behavior later on. Since each and every transition has the potential to get out of control, you will want to establish a routine for each common transition in your classroom. If you would like a list of common transitions, there is one available on page 21.

Classroom activities are academic or non-academic events in your class that aren't transitions. Common examples are participating in a small group discussion, silent reading, or working at centers. You will want to make sure you have a routine in place for any activity which occurs at least once a day (such as turning in homework) and any which tend to cause your students to get out of control (such as emergency drills and assemblies.) If you would like some examples of transitions and classroom activities, you will find a detailed list on page 21.

It is best to proactively prepare your routines before your students arrive on the first day of school, not on the fly as the year progresses. If you don't yet have a job, I suggest you create as many routines as you can. Well-thought-out classroom routines will not only make you a more successful new teacher, it may even give you more confidence in your interviews and help you get a job.

If you have a job and the school year has already started, it's not too late! I suggest you choose your first routine to address a transition or activity that is already driving you a little crazy (possibly from Activity #1) or which takes a lot of class time. Once you have the first situation handled you will have more energy to correct other problems.

Brian and Karen Pick Their Routines

Brian decides to pick a transition—starting the day—because he's tired of taking the first 15 minutes each day trying to get his students to go to their seats and be quiet. He hopes a quiet and orderly start every day will save time, calm his nerves, and engage his students.

It's difficult for Karen to know which routine to pick. She doesn't know which grade level she will teach, what kinds of materials she will be using, or the physical layout of her room. However, Karen does know her ideal teaching style, which is to provide interactive group activities for her students instead of lecturing. She anticipates her students will engage in interactive group activities nearly every day, so she decides to create a routine for how her students will work in groups.

Activity #2

Estimated Time = 5 minutes

Materials

- Pencil or Pen
- Paper
- Template for Activity #2 (page 20)
- Common Transitions and Activities (page 21)

1. Using either paper or the template for this activity, make a list of your own transitions and classroom activities. Once you have created your list, keep it handy and add to it as you think of more.

2. Choose ONE transition or classroom activity to work on for this book. I suggest you choose a transition or activity which causes chaos or wastes a lot of time, or that you envision your students doing at least once a day.

TEMPLATE

Activity #2 ✍

Directions: List some common transitions and activities for your class.

Common Transitions
Starting class*
Ending class*

Common Activities
Listening to the teacher*

* You will always need a routine for this activity.

Activity #2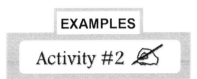

Common Transitions

Entering the Room Before Class	Walking In Line or Passing Time
Returning From Lunch or Recess	Dismissal
Entering the Room After a Pullout	Passing Out Papers
Moving to Carpet Area (Elementary)	Turning In an Assignment
Setting Up for a Lab	Going to Your Locker During Class
Getting Materials Out	Moving Into Centers
Putting Materials Away	Switching Centers
Moving Into Groups	Moving Out of Groups

Common Activities

Correcting Homework	Working at Centers	Free Time
Sharpening Pencils	Cleaning Lockers	Taking a Test
Eating a Snack	Working With a Partner	Using Playground Equipment
Using the Restroom	Working Independently	Cleaning Desks
Drinking Water	Listening to the Teacher	Heading Your Paper
Getting a Bandage	Listening to Another Student	Using Class Computers
Emergency Drills	Participating in a Discussion	Working in Groups
Assemblies	Sharing Materials	Going to the Media Center
Using Paper	Playing Games	Watching a Video
Using Cell Phones	Borrowing the Teacher's Materials	Answering the Intercom or Class Phone

Step 2
Envison Perfection

If you are like many teachers, you may find yourself getting angry at students' misbehavior because you feel they should "know better." When your students don't act the way you expect, you think they are being defiant. For example, I used to get really frustrated when my students would throw books in the bookshelves upside down and backward, resulting in ripped and crumpled pages and missing covers. I thought any fool should know how to put a book away. In reality, many of my students (who were from high-poverty, low-education homes) didn't have books at home. It was up to me to teach them how to care for books.

The truth is, you already have expectations about how you want the students to act, but you may not have thought about them consciously. In order to create a great routine, we first need to discover what we subconsciously expect our students to know how to do.

There are two ways to uncover your subconscious expectations. The first way is to notice what angers or frustrates you about what the students are currently doing, and then picture its opposite. The second is to picture an ideal class or "perfect" student doing the activity.

What Bothers Brian

Since Brian hopes his *Starting the Day* routine will replace what's happening now in his classroom, he decides to pay attention what angers or frustrates him. As his students come into class in the morning, he creates this list of "complaints:"

- They are noisy.
- They bump into each other, argue with each other, and shove each other around.
- They play with toys.
- They get food out of their lunch boxes and eat it.
- They don't use the pencils from the pencil can, but instead use the noisy pencil sharpener.
- They chase each other around.
- They ignore the teacher when it's time to start class.

When Brian writes down each annoying behavior's corresponding positive behavior, it looks like this:

- They use quiet voices (opposite of being noisy.)
- They are considerate of each other's space (opposite of shoving each other.)
- They leave toys at home and food in their backpacks, except for lunch, which they put in the lunch basket.
- They quickly select a pencil from the pencil can.
- They walk at all times.
- They unload their backpacks, turn in their homework, go straight to their desks, and start working on the warm-up.
- They freeze and look at the teacher without talking when the chimes ring.

Now that he's discovered his subconscious expectations, Brian realizes he's never actually taught his students to do these things. He has yelled at them for the behaviors that bother him without explicitly teaching them what he expects. If you discover something similar, try not to beat yourself up about it. The first step to improve your practices is to learn what needs to change. It will take time and energy to change your habits just as much as it will take time for your students' habits to change. Be gentle with yourself as you learn this process.

Define Everything

Notice the first step in Brian's *Starting the Day* routine—use quiet voices. While "use quiet voices" may seem perfectly clear to an adult, your students will likely need some more clarification. Brian's students often shout across the room to each other in the morning, and no matter how often he says to use quiet voices, they continue to yell. The problem is his wording is not defined enough.

When defining physical actions such as entering the classroom, getting out materials, clearing your desk, lining up, going to your seat, and so on, it's often helpful to define, both for yourself and for your students, *how quickly* and *how quietly* you would like the task to be completed. For example, since Brian is obviously unhappy with his students shouting across the room, he needs to figure out what *would* make him happy. Does he want them to be silent? To whisper? To talk in a conversational tone that can only be heard within a three feet of the speaker (sometimes called a three-foot voice?)

Here's Brian's revised list, with more specific definitions. Now that he knows exactly what he wants from his students he will be more prepared to share those expectations with his class.

- Use three-foot voices.
- Don't touch anyone else.
- Walk at all times.
- As soon as you get in the door, take your homework folder and your lunch out of your backpack.
- Immediately put your homework folder in the homework tray and your lunch in the lunch basket.
- Select a pencil from the pencil can in fewer than five seconds.
- Pick up the warm-up assignment and take it straight to your desk
- Work on your assignment without talking.
- When you finish your assignment, read silently at your desk until the teacher rings the chimes.
- When you hear the chimes, look at the teacher without talking.

Since Karen doesn't have a class yet, she decides to picture an ideal class working in groups. She pretends her students are sitting around a table working on a challenging math problem. This is what she sees as she "watches" them.

Karen's Ideal Class

- Students talk politely to each other.
- Students listen to each other.
- Students share materials without fighting.
- Students respect each other's ideas.
- Every student contributes.
- The group stays on task and finishes the assignment.

It's obvious Karen knows exactly what she wants her students to do when they work in groups. However, her list will not be accessible to her students because it assumes the students already know what Karen means by "polite," "on task," "contributes," "respect," and so on. Unfortunately, our students may have been raised by video games and other media, and their idea of "polite" may be very different than ours. Since Karen wants to teach secondary students, she could invite her students to agree together what "respect" looks like. Before she leads that discussion, though, she needs to know what she herself expects.

When trying to get clear about subconscious expectations, I suggest putting the word "how" before each item on your list. In Karen's case, it looks like this:

- HOW do the students talk politely to each other?
- HOW do the students listen to each other?
- HOW do students share materials without fighting?
- HOW do the students respect each other's ideas?
- HOW does every student contribute?

- HOW does the group stay on-task and finish the assignment?

Your answers to these questions will be the key to unlock the *real* expectations underlying your surface expectations. I encourage you to give some real thought to what you actually, deep down, want your students to do. Once you are clear and are able to communicate it to your students, you will be perceived as fair. Students love fair teachers!

Here are Karen's answers to the question "HOW are the students polite to each other?"

- They take turns talking and listen to each other without interrupting.
- They say "please" and "thank you."
- They don't laugh at each other or call each other names.
- If they disagree, they use questions such as "Why do you think…" and "What about…" and "Have you thought of…"

Karen realizes she may need to teach her students how to be polite before she can teach the other steps for working together in groups. She also realizes if the students in her class are reliably polite to each other, it will be helpful not just for group work but for just about every activity she wants to do with her class. She decides to change her routine from *How to Work in Groups* to *How to Have a Polite Discussion*. You may find you need to narrow the focus of your routine as well.

Karen's Expectations for a Polite Discussion

- Include everyone.
- No negative judgment words like "dumb" and "stupid."
- Look at the person who is talking.
- Wait until the other person finishes—don't interrupt.
- If you agree, say so. If you disagree, use clarification questions.
- Stay on topic.

Now that Karen has narrowed her focus, her list is much more specific. This is good, because specific can be taught. Vague can't.

Whether you decide to use the "what angers me" approach or the "ideal class" approach, it is important to be as detailed and specific as possible. Think about *how*. Think about *how quickly* and *how quietly*. And above all, think about how great it's going to be when this activity goes exactly right!

Activity #3

Estimated Time = 20 minutes

Materials

- Pencil or Pen
- Paper
- The Routine From Activity #2
- "What Bothers You" Template (page 32)
- "Ideal Class Exercise" Template (page 33)
- How Quickly and How Quietly Ideas (page 34)

1. Think about the classroom activity you chose for your first routine. Is it bugging you now? If so, use the "What Bothers You" template or a piece of paper, and write down exactly what bothers you about what your class does. What would its opposite behavior be? Write that down, too.

2. If you aren't angry or frustrated, or if you don't yet have your own class, use the "Ideal Class Exercise" template to help you picture the most perfect class in the universe going through this transition or classroom activity (or just make your list on paper.) Exactly what are the students doing? Write it down in specific detail.

3. Look at your list of student actions and ask yourself *how* your students are doing each one. When you notice vague words like *polite*, *quiet*, and *respectful*, ask yourself exactly what that would look like in an ideal world. If they are being polite, exactly *how* are they being polite? If they are being respectful, exactly *how* are they showing respect? Define everything! Make sure to write it down, either on a piece of paper or on the "Ideal Class Exercise" template.

4. If your chosen activity is a set of physical activities such as getting out materials or cleaning the classroom, be sure to include *how quickly* and *how quietly* you would like the students to do these tasks. For a list of ideas for how to communicate *how quickly* and *how quietly* to your students, use the *How Quickly and How Quietly Ideas* template on page 34.

TEMPLATE

Activity #3 ✍

Behavior That Bothers Me	Opposite of That Behavior

TEMPLATE

Activity #3 ✍

What is Your Ideal Class Doing?

Picture the most perfect class in the universe going through this transition or classroom activity. Exactly what are the students doing?

1	
2	
3	
4	
5	
6	

HOW Are They Doing It?

Now ask yourself how. Exactly what does it look like? Define everything! Be sure to include how quickly and how quietly you would like the students to do these tasks.

1	
2	
3	
4	
5	
6	

How Quietly/How Quickly

How Quietly

- Without talking

- Using whisper voices

- So only people within 3 feet of you can hear you (3-foot voices)

- With silent feet

- Talking only to the people right beside you (or at your table)

- Without scraping your chair or desk

- Silently

- Without making a noise

- So quietly that our principal will wonder if the class is even in the room

How Quickly

- Let's see who can be the first to...

- Which table group will be the first to...

- By the time I count to 10

- When I say go. Ready, go!

- In one minute

- In 5 seconds or less

- Faster than the class record (my second period class, the other 5th grade)

- Before the bell rings (secondary)

- By 11:03

- On my count—one (students do step 1), two (students do step 2), three (students do step 3)

- Before the music stops (elementary)

- Faster than me

Step 3 Troubleshooting

Believe it or not, no matter how perfect your plans or how well you teach them, things will go wrong. Not only that, they will go wrong in ways you never even thought about. One purpose of the third step—Troubleshooting—is to anticipate what you can, so you will have the energy to deal with the problems you couldn't anticipate. Troubleshooting is also important because it gives you a chance to make sure you are prepared with all the materials you will need. There are two parts to troubleshooting: imagining ways your routine could go wrong, and physically walking through the routine from the students' point of view.

Imagining What Could Go Wrong

Most teachers who have been in the classroom for awhile don't have any trouble thinking of ways things can go wrong. We lose sleep over it, obsess about it, and/or currently experience it every day. For many of us the difficulty is not in thinking of ways things can go wrong, but in thinking it might even be possible for them to go off without a hitch.

The good news is this negativity, pessimism, and doubt has a place, and this is it! If you have trouble believing a routine can really work because of all the ways the students could mess it up, here is your chance to put that type of thinking to good use.

Think of everything that could go wrong. Make a list. Make a long list if you want. Then for everything you wrote down, think of a way you could fix it. Fixes can be *proactive* or *reactive*. A *proactive fix* is something you do ahead of time to prevent the problem. For instance, if you think your students might forget to bring supplies to class, provide a place they can store the supplies in the classroom or provide a way they can borrow supplies from you.

Another proactive strategy is a *pre-correction* or *explicit prompt*. For example, if you know your students have trouble remembering to raise their hands, remind them about hand-raising before starting a discussion (pre-correction.) During the discussion you could say "raise your hand if you know…" before asking a question (explicit prompt.)

A *reactive strategy* is most likely a consequence or correction. It is best to think of these consequences ahead of time so they will be logical and fair. For older students you can involve them in deciding what is fair. For example, one class decided anyone whose cell phone rang in class would not be allowed to listen to music during independent work time.

Brian's Troubleshooting

Brian found it especially easy to come up with what could go wrong with each step because he already had a list of what was driving him crazy. He used that as a starting point and also added a few more items. Here is his entire list, including his new additions:

- Running
- Playing with toys
- Getting out food and eating it
- Pushing/shoving/arguing
- Yelling
- Not getting to work
- 3-5 students at a time ask the teacher questions
- Backpacks thrown on the floor
- Lunches still in backpacks
- Homework not turned in/lost

Brian's Proactive Fixes

- **Pushing/shoving/arguing**—Teach hands to self and how to take turns.
- **Yelling**—Teach students how to use three-foot voices; meet students at the door and remind them of noise expectations before they enter the room.
- **Backpacks thrown on the floor**—Teach students how to hang up backpacks.

Brian's Reactive Fixes

- **Running**—Students who run practice walking at recess.
- **Playing with toys**—Toys confiscated and returned at the end of the day.
- **Not getting to work**—Recognize immediate starters with token and/or verbal praise.
- **Backpacks thrown on the floor**—Dismiss students at the end of the day using backpacks that are hanging up.
- **Lunches still in backpacks**—Dismiss students for lunch by picking lunchboxes that are in the right place.
- **Homework not turned in/lost**—Extra game time for all students who turn in the week's work. The rest of the students finish homework during game time.

Karen's Troubleshooting

Karen drew upon her experience as a substitute teacher to help her think about what could go wrong with a class discussion. Here's what she came up with:

- 1-2 students dominate the discussion
- Name-calling
- Students interrupt each other and shout each other down
- Contradictions and rude disagreements
- Off-topic conversations

Karen's Proactive Fixes

- **1-2 students dominate the discussion**—Appoint a facilitator or utilize a "talking stick;" require students to either share or pass before moving on to the next question or topic.
- **Name-calling**—Teach students ahead of time which specific names will not be tolerated.
- **Contradictions and rude disagreements**—Explicitly teach students acceptable ways to disagree, and have a discussion about this.

Karen's Reactive Fixes

- **Name-calling**—Zero tolerance; detention on first violation.

- **Interrupting**—Have a fun penalty for interrupting, such as having to sing the school song or bring candy the next day. The teacher also has to do the penalty if she interrupts.

- **Off-topic conversations**—Use the fun penalty for this, too.

Physical Walk-Through

After you have thought through anything that can go wrong with your routine, it's helpful to physically walk through your routine as if you were a student, noting trouble spots and materials needed. Actually sit in a student desk and try to do the routine. Notice physical barriers, distractions, and obstacles. Make sure you have everything available the students will need. When you physically walk through the routine you will notice things about your classroom that surprise you.

For example, as Brian walks through the door of his classroom he almost bumps into a table. He realizes part of the reason his students shove each other is the bottleneck area by the door. He solves this problem by moving the table.

As he moves toward the backpack area, he notices part of the area is hidden from view by a bookshelf. He realizes some of the problems in the backpack area are caused because he can't see students and intervene to help them solve problems. He moves the bookshelf.

Next he notices there aren't enough hooks for the backpacks. This solves the mystery of why so many students throw their backpacks on the floor. He makes a note to install some hooks when he gets a chance. In the meantime he decides to ask a few responsible students to hang their backpacks on their chairs.

As he walks through the rest of his routine, Brian makes a few more changes to streamline his process and facilitate traffic flow and make it easier. For the first time in a long time, he feels it might be possible to start the day with quiet and order instead of noise and chaos.

Karen, of course, can't do a physical walk-through yet. She will do it after she gets a job as she sets up her room and plans her first week.

Activity #4

Estimated Time = 20 minutes

Materials

- Pencil or Pen
- Your Routine from Activity #2
- Pessimistic Attitude (so you can think about what could go wrong)
- Your Classroom (for the walk-through) or your imagination if you don't have a classroom
- Troubleshooting Template (from page 44)

1. Proactively think about what could go wrong with your routine. If you are like Karen and don't have a classroom yet, simply use your imagination and/or ask another teacher to help you brainstorm.

2. If you have a classroom, pretend to be a student doing the routine. If you discover any physical barriers or distractions, remove them or plan ways around them.

3. While you do the walk-through, list any materials needed for your routine.

TEMPLATE

Activity #4

Directions: Think about what could go wrong with your routine. In your classroom, pretend to be a student doing the routine. If you discover any physical barriers or distractions, remove them or plan ways around them. While you do the walk-through, make a note of any materials needed for your routine.

What Could Go Wrong	How to Fix It

Materials Needed

Step 4
Lesson Planning

By now every aspect of the routine should be crystal clear to you. You have gathered all the materials, prepared the physical space, and figured out explicitly what you want (and what you don't.) The only thing left is to teach the routine to your students. Since you've put so much time and energy into creating your routine, you definitely want to make sure it's a success when you teach it to your students. The best way to do this is take the time to make an actual lesson plan.

You'll notice the process of teaching your routine is similar to teaching academics—it needs to be done systematically and with a definite purpose in mind. Here are the key components of the lesson:

- Topic (overview of the activity)
- Rationale (why the activity is important)
- Direct Instruction (demonstration)
- Guided Practice
- Independent Practice and Evaluation
- Re-Teach as Needed

Topic (Overview of the Activity)

The topic of your lesson plan is easy—it's just the name of the activity you've been working with this whole time. For Brian it's *Starting the Day*. For Karen it's *How to Have a Polite Discussion*.

Rationale (Why the Activity Is Important)

The next part of your lesson—communicating to the students why this routine is important—may take a little more thought. If you want to inspire your students to follow your routine, you need to be able to explain why it's important to *them*, not to you. If you feel comfortable, you could ask for student input by asking them to explain why it is important to know how to do the activity. Whether or not you ask for student input, emphasize what this routine will do *for your students*.

For example, Brian's routine is important to *him* because he doesn't want to get a headache every day while wasting a ton of instructional time, but it's important for his third grade students to feel safe and taken care of. So Brian's rationale will be about his students knowing their backpack is safe and being able to find their lunch at lunchtime. He will also talk about how great the students will feel when they start their day in a calm, peaceful, relaxed way.

Brian worries about teaching the students how to enter the room halfway through the year. He doesn't want to appear incompetent or weak. He also doesn't want it to seem like he's blaming the students. He decides to use this wording (feel free to modify it for your own Rationale.)

Over the weekend I realized I've never actually taught this class the best way to enter the classroom each day. It's important for us to get off to a good start each day so we can learn as much as possible in the short amount of time we have together. It's also important for you to know where your backpack is and where your lunch is so you can get ready for lunch on time. Today I am going to show you the routine for entering the classroom, and we are going to use this routine from now on.

Karen's routine about how to have a polite discussion is important to *her* because she doesn't want to deal with bickering, disrespect, and noninvolvement in her classroom. Her high school students don't care so much about that, but they do care deeply about fairness and self-expression. In order to inspire her students, Karen will need to talk to her students about how this routine will give everyone a fair chance to express their opinions and be heard.

Direct Instruction (Demonstration)

In the direct instruction portion of the lesson, you run through how to do the activity, demonstrate the most common things that can go wrong, and demonstrate your fixes. When you demonstrate how to do the activity correctly, use your *Ideal Class* chart from Activity #3 as a reference for yourself. Show the students where to get needed materials and any other details they might need to know. Refer to your *Troubleshooting Template* while you demonstrate common mistakes and how to correct them.

Guided Practice

Most people learn best by doing, so your students will need time to practice the routine. If possible, have each student practice one at a time. Depending upon how long the activity takes, you will need to provide something else for the rest of the class to do. Also, it is best for students to practice in the environment where they will be using the routine. For example, they practice assembly behavior in the auditorium or multipurpose room and lunchtime behavior in the lunchroom. If you have a reward system in place in your classroom, this is a perfect place to use it. If you don't have a formal reward system, you will still want to provide plenty of positive acknowledgement as your students successfully practice the routine.

Brian and Karen's Guided Practice

After demonstrating the *Entering the Room* routine, Brian asks the students to practice it one or two at a time while the rest of the class reads silently. He offers the prize of going to lunch one minute early if everyone gets it right.

After Karen teaches her students how to have a polite discussion, she plans to lead a whole-class getting-to-know-you discussion. During the discussion, she plans to monitor whether or not the students are able to follow the *How to Have a Polite Discussion* guidelines. If she notices students forgetting some of the components, she will politely correct them and/or provide a time for the students to receive extra coaching from her until they get it right.

Independent Practice and Evaluation

Independent practice is an opportunity for the students to perform the routine while you monitor to make sure each student gets it. Mastery is the goal, so re-teach individuals and groups as needed or have students teach and remind each other. If you have a rewards system utilize it during independent practice. You may also need to introduce some logical consequences, such as asking your students to practice the routine during passing time or lunch.

For Brian's class, independent practice will occur as they enter the room the following day. Before dismissing his class for the day, Brian reviews the expectations for entering the room the next day and offers a reward if everyone does it correctly. The next day before letting his students in the room, he reminds them he will be testing to see who remembers what to do. Although most students do well, a few forget some key steps. Brian goes over those steps with only those students during their recess time.

For her independent practice, Karen plans to ask the students to have an actual small group discussion about what they like and hate about math. She plans roam the room during the discussion with a list of students and check off any who demonstrate they know how to have a polite discussion. If the entire class is successful, they will be allowed to listen to music during an individual assignment.

Brian's and Karen's completed lesson plans are included with the next activity, if you would like to modify them to use with your class.

Activity #5 ✍

Estimated Time = 10 minutes

Materials

- Pencil or Pen
- Your Routine From Activity #3
- Lesson Plan Template (page 52)
- Karen's Lesson Plan—*How to Have a Polite Discussion (Secondary)* (page 53)
- Brian's Lesson Plan—*Starting the Day (Third Grade)* (page 54)

1. Utilize the work you have already done to flesh out your lesson plan. Please write it down so you can use it year after year.

2. If necessary, refer back to the appropriate section of this book while you create your lesson plan. You may also want to ask for input from other teachers or email me at PositiveTeachingStrategies@gmail.com.

LESSON PLAN TEMPLATE

Activity #5 ✍

Topic (overview of activity)

Rationale (importance of activity TO THE STUDENTS)

Direct Instruction (demonstrate the following)

Step or Component	What Could Go Wrong And How to Fix It

Guided Practice Activity

Independent Practice and Evaluation

KAREN'S LESSON PLAN

Activity #5 ✍

Topic (overview of activity)

How to have a polite discussion

Rationale (importance of activity TO THE STUDENTS)

It's important for everyone to be respected and listened to, and to get to say what they want. It's only fair! Also, I don't want you to have to listen to me talking for the whole class. I want you to be able to work with your friends in groups.

Direct Instruction (demonstrate the following)

Step or Component	What Could Go Wrong And How to Fix It
Include everyone.	**1-2 students dominate**—Require everyone to either talk or pass before moving on; use a "talking stick;" appoint a facilitator
No negative judgment words like "dumb" and "stupid."	**Name-calling**—Zero tolerance—detention on first violation; teach explicitly, including names/words that are not allowed
Look at the person who is talking.	**Looking away**—Teach explicitly. Practice.
Wait until the other person finishes—don't interrupt.	**Students interrupt each other and shut each other down**—Use "talking stick;" teach turn-taking; fun penalty for violations that the teacher is also subject to
If you agree, say so. If you don't, use clarifying questions.	**Contradictions and rude disagreements**—Explicitly teach acceptable ways to disagree; ask students for input.
Stay on topic.	**Off-topic conversations**—Reminders; use the fun penalty for this one, too.

Guided Practice Activity

Whole class getting-to-know-you discussion using the talking stick. Reminders for students who struggle; extra (non-class) practice time for individuals who need extra coaching.

Independent Practice and Evaluation

Group discussion about what you like and hate about math. Teacher circulates, observes, and corrects when needed.

BRIAN'S LESSON PLAN

Activity #5 ✍

Topic (overview of activity)

Starting the Day (Third Grade)

Rationale (importance of activity TO THE STUDENTS)

Over the weekend I realized I've never actually taught this class the best way to enter the classroom each day. It's important for us to get off to a good start each day so we can learn as much as possible in the short amount of time we have together. It's also important for you to know where your backpack is and where your lunch is so you can get ready for lunch on time. Today I am going to show you the routine for entering the classroom, and we are going to use this routine from now on.

Direct Instruction (demonstrate the following)

Step or Component	What Could Go Wrong And How to Fix It
Use 3-foot voice.	**Yelling**—Teach 3-foot voice. Remind class before letting them in. Re-teach and practice at recess if voices get too loud
Don't touch anyone else.	**Pushing/shoving/arguing**—Teach hands to self expectations; practice how to take turns and wait for others
Walk at all times.	**Running**—Explicitly teach walking expectation; practice at recess if students persist in running
As soon as you get in the door, take your homework folder and lunch out of backpack and hang up backpack.	**Backpacks thrown on the floor; Playing with toys or eating food from lunch**—Install more hooks; Teach that only lunches and homework folder come out of backpack; toys and food confiscated & returned later
Immediately put your homework folder in the homework tray	**Homework not turned in/lost**—Extra game time for students who turn in all their work; finish/get help during game time if not completed
Immediately put your lunch in the lunch basket.	**Lunches still in backpacks**—Dismiss to lunch by drawing lunches out of basket
Select a pencil from the pencil can in fewer than 5 seconds	**Using pencil sharpener**—Ensure pencil can is full; re-teach procedure at recess if needed
Pick up the warm-up assignment and take it straight to your desk.	**Wandering; going to desk without assignment**—Extra practice at recess if needed; verbally recognize those who remember.
Work on your assignment without talking.	**Not getting to work**—Recognize immediate starters with token/verbal praise
When the teacher rings the chimes, look at the teacher without talking.	**Continuing to read; talking**—Whole class reward if done correctly.

Guided Practice Activity

Two students at a time practice entry procedure during silent reading.

Independent Practice and Evaluation

Evaluate students as they practice the next day of school. Re-teach and re-direct as necessary.

Teach the Routine

The final step in the process is to actually teach your routine to your students. Here is how I suggest you roll it out.

1. Explain (or lead a discussion about) the importance *to the students* of learning this routine.

2. Describe in specific detail how to do the routine. Model each step (show, don't just tell.)

3. Explain and model things that can go wrong while doing the routine. Explain and model how to avoid those things or fix them if they happen. One fun way to do this is to deliberately mess up doing the routine and ask the students to tell you where the mistake(s) occurred.

4. Ask the students to practice doing the routine, making sure they have all had a chance to try it. Correct any mistakes you see and recognize, reinforce, and reward your students when they do it correctly.

5. Provide a time for the students to practice the routine independently, and make sure each student can do it.

Do not make the common mistake of attempting to teach a classroom routine or procedure five minutes before you need it. For example, sometimes teachers attempt to teach their students how to line up five minutes before the class is supposed to be somewhere. This is a huge mistake! It will take much longer to teach the procedure the first time than it actually takes to do the procedure. For instance, it might take 30 minutes to teach the students how to line up the first time. Once they know how, they should be able to line up in less than a minute.

I can hear the objections now. "30 minutes! I can't take 30 minutes for each one-minute procedure!" I understand it's difficult to find time in your busy schedule, but you need to realize how much time you will be saving in the long run. If I don't invest the 30 minutes to teach my students how to line up, it will probably take them at least 10 minutes each and every time they need to do it. Assuming they line up four times a day (recess, specials, lunch, and going home) I will save 36 minutes *every day*. Even if they don't line up perfectly each time, and even if we need to review from time to time (and we will) I will still easily get back the 30 minutes I invested in that lesson in just the first week. In addition, both my students and I will be less stressed out.

Finally, you will want to plan some time for review. Especially as the students are first learning the routine, you will need to make sure to review the steps with them often. You will also need to review your routine after weekends, holidays, and school breaks. Your review lessons will not take as long as the initial lesson. For example, I would probably review my lining up lesson for five minutes each time my students line up on the first day, then for one minute each time on the second day. The following Monday, I would go back to a five-minute review the first time they need to line up, with a one-minute review for the rest of the day. Then I would spot-review as needed.

I recommend teaching a routine like Brian's for the first time in the afternoon, preferably on the first day of school. A routine like Karen's will probably take most of a 45-minute period to teach. She should plan to teach it the day before she wants her students to work in groups for the first time.

Activity #6

Estimated Time = 5 minutes

Materials

- Pencil or Pen
- Lesson Plan Book or Calendar

1. Look at your calendar or lesson plan book and block out a logical time to teach your routine. Make sure to allow more time than you think it will take and have a filler activity ready in case your students learn the routine more quickly than you expect.

2. If you don't yet have your own class, make up a generic schedule for the first week of school and figure out where your routine would likely fit in. Once you get your own class you can adapt it to fit your actual schedule.

Next Steps

Do you remember the first activity in this book? I asked you to write down five things that worry or bother you about student behavior in your classroom. Take a look back at your list and realize you now have the power to solve them! The time invested in just this one routine will pay you back over and over again throughout the school year.

Now that you've finished your routine, the next step is to create another one. You will probably be able to create your second routine in about half the time it took you to create this one. Your third one will be even faster. After you create routines for every major activity in your classroom you will be able to use them over and over again, year after year.

Congratulations on all you have accomplished and best wishes to you as you do the most important work there is—teaching.

ABOUT THE AUTHOR

Katrina Ayres is a certified teacher with more than 20 years of experience teaching elementary and secondary students in both rural and urban settings. She first discovered the importance of classroom management during her disastrous first teaching assignment in rural Hawaii, which she talks about in her first book, *All the Ways I Screwed Up My First Year of Teaching, and How You Can Avoid Doing It, Too,* available on Amazon.

Through her own experiences and with the help of mentors along the way, Katrina discovered what really works in the classroom. She is now on a mission to share what she has learned through her workshops, seminars, books, boot camps, coaching, and mentoring. You can reach her at PositiveTeachingStrategies@gmail.com or on her website at PositiveTeachingStrategies.com.

Katrina lives with her husband (who is also a teacher) and her cat (who is not) in a shiny glass building in Portland, Oregon.

Made in the USA
Columbia, SC
29 December 2017